Affirmations for the soul

Wendy Middlehurst

Affirmations for the soul

Affirmations for the soul

ISBN: 9781077410459

Affirmations for the soul

Affirmations have been used for centuries, quite possibly even longer. To 'affirm' something means to declare it as true, make a statement of something or also, in some uses of the word, to encourage or support.

They are very *very* powerful things. I was using affirmations to control my anxiety around going to work in a job I really hated before I even knew what an affirmation was. I would repeat over and over again on the drive there…

'Everything will be ok. You can do this job. The time will pass quickly. You can do this!"

You might have created your own similar affirmations at times too.

When you hear something over and over again you start to believe it – so be very careful indeed about what goes on in your head.

Your thoughts are powerful things indeed.

I've created this collection of affirmations for you. All of them have been created with the intention that they will calm and uplift you and to help you to remember your worth.

Read them aloud or in your head – either is fine, although I do find that saying them out loud or even writing them down adds power to them.

Read them as often as possible. Commit them to memory if you can. The more often you use them the more their words will filter into your everyday thought processes and calm and uplift you throughout the day.

Either go through the book reading a different one each day or just flick through and pick one at random., it's totally up to you.

You could even try writing your own too.

Enjoy!

♥

Morning affirmations

As I breathe in, I give thanks for this day.

As I breathe out, I release any unwanted energy
that no longer serves me.

I imagine myself bathed in sunlight.

The sunlight strengthens me and prepares me for
the day ahead.

I am supported.

I am protected.

I am strong.

I am at peace with myself and the world around
me.

I am safe.

I am loved.

I am worthy.

And so it is.

♥

This morning I give thanks for a new day.

I release any energy that no longer serves me.

I see myself surrounded by sunshine and beautiful
white light.

I breathe in faith & trust in the universe.

I breathe out fear, pessimism and doubt.

I breathe in trust, peace, optimism and love.

I am ready to begin.

I welcome this new day.

I know I am always supported.

And so it is.

This morning I give thanks for a new day.

I release any unhelpful & unwanted energy from the night.

I release anything that no longer serves me.

I see myself surrounded by sunshine and beautiful white light.

The light and warmth of the sun clears my energy field and re-energizes me.

I am ready to begin.

I welcome this new day.

And so it is.

♥

I am thankful to have been blessed with another day.

I breathe in thanks for safety as I slept.

I breathe out any left-over fear or negativity from the previous day.

I am supported.

I am blessed.

I am loved.

Today will be all I hope it to be.

Today will be full of smiles from strangers & unexpected support.

I breathe in thanks

I breathe out doubt.

I trust in the protection that is always around me.

I am in alignment with my soul.

And so it is.

♥

This morning I breathe in connection to universal source energy.

I breathe out fear, a sense of detachment from the universe and mistrust.

I breathe in peace.

I breathe out anger and hate.

I breathe in joy and wonder.

I breathe out sadness & pain.

I feel myself surrounded by the arms of the universe.

I feel myself wrapped in unconditional love and protective energy.

I feel completely supported.

Completely grounded.

Completely safe.

I welcome this day ahead.

I welcome miracles and I receive them openly

I am thankful to start a new day

And so it is

♥

On waking I give thanks for safety as I slept

I give thanks to be alive and I am grateful for
another day.

I am wrapped in calming, white light.

I am wrapped in love and protection – always.

I am filled with strength.

I am filled with peace.

I am filled with thanks.

As I start this day, I welcome abundance of all
kinds into my life.

I open myself up to receive all the blessings
prepared for me.

I give thanks for all that I have,

I know that I am always protected, supported and
loved.

Always

And so it is

This morning I release all unhelpful energies from the previous day and the previous night.

I dissolve any negative energy around me.

I imagine any negative energy around me dissolving and dispersing into the vastness of the universe. And as it disappears it is transformed into stardust.

In its place I welcome in beautiful white, healing light from source.

I imagine the light filling me with strength,

With courage,

And a remembrance of who I really am.

Of how strong I really am.

And how talented I really am.

As I am held in this protective space of white light and source energy

I remember what I'm made of.

I remember I'm part of the universe.

I remember that I am safe,

supported and loved unconditionally every single second.

And so it is.

This morning I breathe in thanks for this new day.

I breathe out worry, doubt and fear.

I breathe in the stillness of the early morning.

I breathe out stress and busyness.

I am safe in the arms of the universe.

I am surrounded by angels.

I am loved unconditionally.

I am stronger than I remember.

I am ready to begin.

And so it is.

♥

This morning I breathe in and remember the truth
of what I am.

I am a soul.

I breathe out and release all my doubts and fears.

I breathe in complete trust in myself.

I breathe out all doubt.

I am a soul.

I am strong.

I am wise.

I am connected to the Universe.

I have all the answers.

I have all the knowledge.

I know what steps to take.

And so it is.

♥

This morning I grateful to be alive.

I breathe in hope, faith and positivity.

I breathe out worry, fear and pessimism.

I am calm.

I am supported.

I am safe in the arms of the universe.

I am loved unconditionally.

I am stronger than I remember.

I am ready to begin.

And so it is.

♥

Today I am thankful for all that I have.

Today I notice the breath in my lungs and the beating of my heart.

Today I am thankful that I have a fresh new day.

I open myself to possibility that today will be full of miracles.

Today I invite love in.

Today I accept all the blessings that the universe wishes to shower me with.

And so it is.

This morning I send calming energy from the top of my head to the soles of my feet.

As the energy moves down it relaxes each muscle one by one.

I am calm.

I am safe.

I am ready.

I breathe in knowledge that today will be a good day.

I breathe out fear and negative predictions.

I breathe in love, hope, joy and trust.

I breathe out fear, anger, pessimism and doubt.

I am ready for today.

And so it is

This morning I imagine myself wrapped in a
blanket of love and peace.

I imagine the blanket shimmers like crystals and is
all colours of the rainbow.

The blanket warms me and reminds me that I am
strong.

That I am safe.

And that I am fully supported.

Always

And so it is.

🖤

I start today knowing everything is working out
for me.

Trusting that I am always supported.

Trusting that I can cope with anything today
brings.

Knowing the strength I possess and the love that
surrounds me.

Today I start my day calm,

Peaceful,

Thankful.

I am enough.

And so it is

🖤

This morning I stretch as much as I can.

I feel the energy awakening in my body.

I feel myself gathering my strength for the day.

I know I can face whatever today brings me.

I align myself to my soul.

I remember I am made from stardust.

I remember my power.

I am ready to begin.

🖤

Today I tell myself how well I am doing.

Today I remind myself of all the challenges I have navigated in my life.

Today I am thankful for the wisdom and lessons learned.

Today I intend to help another person.

I intend to smile at each person I meet.

I intend to be my true self.

And to travel through this day with joy.

And so it is.

♥

As I wake up, I give thanks for all that I have.

All that I know.

All the experiences I have had.

I give thanks for the wisdom of my soul.

I give thanks for the universal source energy that surrounds me.

I remember that I co-create this universe.

I focus on feelings of love, joy and abundance and welcome in more of the same.

And so it is.

🖤

Today I release all energy that no longer serves
me.

I open myself up to receive abundance.

I open myself up to receive joy.

I open myself up to receive happiness.

I open myself up to welcome in love.

Today I intend to accept all compliments I receive
with grace and to give as many back as I receive.

I start the day knowing I am fully supported and
loved.

Always.

♥

Today I accept myself for who I am.

Today I am proud of me.

Today I am taking care of me.

Today I am my own best friend.

Today I am my own loudest cheerleader.

Today will be a great day.

♥

This morning I breathe in and feel beautiful life force energy all around me.

I breathe out all worry & fear.

I welcome in support.

I welcome in abundance.

I welcome in love.

I release any blocks to my receiving.

I breathe in complete faith and trust that everything is always working out for me.

I am ready to begin my day with joy.

And so it is.

Any time affirmations

As I breathe in, I remember there is greatness in me.

I breathe out doubt and fear.

I breathe in and remember I am here on purpose.

I breathe out doubt and fear.

I am talented.

I am unlimited potential.

I am strength.

I am wisdom.

I am knowledge.

I am supported by all that is good in the universe.

Always.

And so it is.

I am safe.

I am supported.

I am held.

I place my feet flat on the earth.

I am held safe here by Mother Nature.

I breathe in deeply, and exhale slowly.

I return to calm.

I return to relaxed.

All is well

And so it is.

I am strong.

I am wise.

I am knowledgeable.

I am talented.

I am me.

I am unique.

I am loved.

Always

All that I am is always enough.

I have nothing to prove to anyone but myself.

Other people's opinions of me are none of my business.

I am safe.

I am supported.

I hear my soul's desires and take action,

knowing everything is always working out for me exactly as it should for my highest good.

And so it is

♥

Everything is always working out for me.

Exactly as it should.

I trust.

I have faith.

I am safe.

I breathe in and remember that everything is
always working out for me.

I breathe out and release all my worries.

I remember I am supported.

I remember I am powerful.

I remember I am here on purpose, with a purpose.

I release anything that no longer serves me.

I reconnect with my soul.

I breathe in love.

I breathe out fear.

All will be well.

And so it is.

♥

I am strong.

I am fierce.

I am focussed.

I know what I want.

I know what steps to take.

I trust the guidance of my soul.

Always.

Today I release my worries and fears.

Today I connect with my heart and soul.

Today I hold the vision of all that I desire.

And give thanks for all that I have.

I am protected.

I am empowered.

I am me.

I am enough.

I am not afraid to shine.

And so it is.

♥

When I am going through hell I remember to keep going.

I continue inch by inch.

I am kind to myself.

I am patient with myself.

I support myself.

I am my own best friend.

My loudest cheerleader.

My eternal support.

I can achieve whatever I desire.

All will be well.

And so it is.

I breathe in and I smile.

Wherever I am, whatever I'm doing – I smile.

And I breathe.

Long, slow, deep breaths.

Believing that something wonderful is always
around the corner.

Good things are supposed to happen to me.

I am worthy.

I am deserving.

I am loved.

Deeply and wholeheartedly, I am loved by the
universe and by myself.

Good things are supposed to happen to me.

Good things do happen to me.

So I smile.

And so it is.

I am enough.

I trust my own inner guidance.

I know I am the expert in me.

I have the answers.

I know the next step to take.

I always make the most soul aligned decisions.

I am in control.

All will be well.

And so it is.

♥

I am worthy.

I am perfect as I am.

I am worthy of all I desire.

No-one is any better or worse than me.

I am loved.

I allow myself to receive love.

I show love to others.

I am grateful for the energy of love and for the
wonders it creates.

And so it is.

There is greatness in me.

I am here on purpose.

With a purpose.

My soul knows it.

I breathe in, and I listen to its message.

I breathe out fear and the chattering of the
conditioned mind.

I connect to soul.

It knows the way.

I trust it.

I trust myself.

All is well.

I have the answers.

I know the answers.

I trust my answers.

Always.

♥

I breathe in and align with my higher self.

I remember my strength.

I breathe out and let go of the idea that I am
disconnected to source energy.

I know I am connected.

I know I am a co-creator of the universe.

My life can become however I want it to be.

I can achieve my goals.

My vision can become reality.

I hold the vision.

I believe in the vision.

I trust it will be delivered.

I know I am worthy of all I desire.

I let go of impatience.

I trust it will be.

And so it is.

Right now, I breathe in and allow my muscles to relax.

I notice where I have been carrying tension in my body.

I stretch this area and release the stress I was carrying.

I listen to the sounds around me.

I notice the temperature around me.

I focus on simply my breath.

I place a hand on my heart and give thanks for the amazing gift of a human body.

And I give thanks for the support I receive daily from the universe.

I allow myself to feel loved and know I am supported.

Always.

♥

I am proud of who I am.

I am proud of all that I have achieved.

I can do anything I set my mind to.

I have more strength, abilities and power than I can ever imagine.

And I am supported by all that is good in the universe – always.

I have nothing to fear.

I am on the right track.

I trust that everything is always working out for me.

I take action to move me in the direction of my dreams and I expect miracles.

And so it is.

♥

♥

Evening

affirmations

I place my hand on my heart and offer thanks for
the experiences of the day – good and bad.

I am grateful for the strength I possess to face all
my challenges.

I breathe in the energy of the moon and stars.

Their light fuels my soul and restores my strength.

I breathe in peace, love and healing.

I breathe out fear, anger and doubt.

I trust I am supported.

I trust my angels, guides and ancestors draw near.

I trust that they strengthen me when I need it.

I am strong.

I am calm.

I am loved.

Unconditionally loved.

Always.

Tonight, I release any unhelpful & unwanted
energy of the day.

I breathe in the universal love that is available to
me always.

I release any energy connected to me that belongs
to others.

I breathe in peace.

I am surrounded by love.

Always.

And so it is.

♥

I breathe in and offer thanks for this day.

As I breathe out, I release all unwanted energy from the day.

I imagine myself bathed in moon and starlight.

I am safe.

I am held by the arms of the universe.

I am protected.

I am worthy.

I am loved.

Always.

🖤

Tonight, I release any unhelpful & unwanted
energy of the day.

I release anything that no longer serves me.

My energy field is clear.

I breathe in peace, love & light.

I am surrounded by love.

I am refreshed & renewed, ready for tomorrow.

And so it is.

This evening I release all that no longer serves me.

I release any unhelpful energy.

I release the stresses and strains of the day.

I breathe in hope.

I breathe out fear.

I breathe in love.

I breathe out doubt.

I am safe in the arms of the universe,

held and protected always.

My heart is filled with gratitude for my many blessings.

Each breath is a blessing.

I am strong.

I am safe.

I am protected.

I am loved.

♥

Tonight, I am thankful for all that I have.

I breathe in calm and peace.

I breathe out all the worries and stress I have
collected today.

I breathe in trust.

I breathe out doubt.

I am thankful to be who I am.

I am thankful for the talents that I have.

I know I have greatness within me.

Tomorrow will be a good day.

And so it is

As I prepare to sleep, I am reminded of what I really am.

I remember the power I possess.

The strength I possess.

The wisdom I possess.

I remember I am a child of the universe.

A co-creator of this wonderful world.

I am safe.

I am supported.

Everything is unfolding exactly as it should for my highest good.

I trust in the universe.

I trust in myself.

I am thankful for this day I have lived and the experiences it has offered me.

I welcome tomorrow and give thanks for today.

And so it is.

♥

This evening I allow my thoughts to drift to all the blessings that I have.

To the things that went well today.

To the things that I am lucky to have.

To the fact that I am loved unconditionally.

I allow myself to feel peace,

Calm,

Thanks,

Hope,

Love.

I am thankful to be alive.

I am ready to sleep and recharge.

I am ready to start again tomorrow.

And so it is.

🖤

Tonight, I shake off any energy that isn't my own.

Anything unwanted and unhelpful that has clung to my energy field today.

I imagine a wave of loving and helpful energy washing over me, taking with it anything that no longer serves me.

I am cleansed.

I am recharged.

I am filled with peaceful, calming, loving energy.

I am ready to sleep.

Knowing I am held in the arms of the universe.

Knowing everything is working out for my highest good.

And so it is.

Tonight, I remember I am strong.

I remember I am worthy.

I remember I am capable.

I remember I am a co-creator of the universe.

I cleanse my energy.

I protect my energy.

I ground myself.

And I fill my dreams with all that I desire,
knowing it is all possible.

And so it is.

♥

This evening I allow myself to rest full.

I let go of the need to be busy.

I remember that relaxing is actually productive.

I allow myself to just be present.

To be in this moment.

To know that all is well in this moment.

And so it is.

♥

Tonight, I close my eyes and allow myself to relax.

I give myself permission to relax.

I breathe in calm.

I breathe out stress.

I am safe.

I place one hand on my heart and tell myself that everything I did today was enough,

I am enough,

I have always been enough.

And so it is.

Tonight, I let myself remember all the things that went well today.

All the times I succeeded.

All the times I overcame challenges.

And I congratulate myself for carrying on.

I am proud of myself.

I am in awe of myself.

Every day.

And so it is.

I am worthy of receiving blessings.

I am worthy of receiving abundance.

I expect miracles.

I know that good things are supposed to happen
to me.

I trust that they do.

And I am thankful for all that I receive.

♥

This evening, I take a moment to stand outside
and look up at the sky.

I allow my soul to feel deeply connected to
vastness of the universe.

I remember what I am a part of.

I remember just how amazing this universe is.

I remember how little I know with the logical
mind, and instead trust what I feel in my heart and
my soul.

That I am here on purpose.

That there is greatness in me.

That I am magical.

That I am fully supported.

That I am free.

♥

This evening I am safe,

I am supported,

I am held.

I have complete faith and trust in myself and in
my own capabilities.

I have the answers.

My path is unfolding exactly as it should.

All will be well.

And so it is.

♥

With each breath in, my strength increases.

With each breath out my fear decreases.

This evening I allow my face to be illuminated by the moonlight.

I let it's gentle glow soak into my energy field.

With each breath in, the moonlight dissolves any sadness, hurt or fear.

And with each breath out I allow myself to release any stress and unhelpful energy from today.

I am cleansed.

I am relaxed.

I am ready to sleep.

And so it is.

Tonight, I set aside all my fears and worries.

I breathe in and allow myself to drift into the realms of my imagination.

I allow myself to explore all the positive possibilities.

To explore all the possible miraculous scenarios.

To explore the possibility that absolutely anything is possible.

I immerse myself in this realm and soak up its positive and uplifting energy.

I know I can come to this place whenever I need to.

It is always available to me.

Always.

And so it is.

I breathe in calm.

I breath out fear.

I breathe in peace.

I breathe out doubt.

I breathe in love.

I breathe out hate.

I am supported.

I am worthy.

I receive abundance daily.

I am enough.

And so it is.

🖤

Connect with the author

I'd love for you to follow my books on
Instagram:
www.instagram.com/soulpagejournals

Or my business page on Facebook;
https://www.facebook.com/Soul-Page-
Holistics-873724666156497/

You are very welcome to join my fabulous
group,
The Soul Searchers Movement
here;
https://www.facebook.com/groups/4061570
26812682/

You are also very welcome to email me at
soulpageholistics@gmail.com

I look forward to hearing from you and
connecting with you. If you have enjoyed this
book, I would be extremely grateful if you
could leave a review on Amazon.
Thank you & lots of love

Wendy x

Affirmations for the soul

♥

Printed in Poland
by Amazon Fulfillment
Poland Sp. z o.o., Wrocław

51027159R00043